Ebbs, Flows, & Love

Stephanie Lauryn Johnson

BookLeaf Publishing

Presentation by *BookLeaf Publishing*

Web: www.bookleafpub.com

E-mail: info@bookleafpub.com

ISBN: 9789357211406

First edition 2022

DEDICATION

To EVERYONE I Love & I Love EVERYONE.

PREFACE

She never thought of herself as strong or independent. She always felt soft, weak, and like a complete push over no mater how she looked on the outside. She mentally broke at the thought of being judged by those who never really knew much about her. Misunderstood, she felt as though she never fit in with any crowd since birth. Family included. Hid behind books, and released her tension wit a pen and a pad writing everything from what was in her mind down to her heart. She wrote to release ever since she learned to write a full sentence. She had no knowledge of any other avenue to release her mental struggles. At one point she wanted nothing more than to fit in and be understood. To feel like she belonged and for those around her to love her for her. THEN SHE AWOKE and realized it all starts from within. Until she created unconditional love, peace, bliss and self acceptance inside herself nothing else mattered. She began to care less about what "they" thought and more about getting to know herself. She stopped caring or wondering what anyone else felt about her. Made herself feel special.

Understood the level of her own worth. She knew no other soul was a guarantee, but she could always be there for herself. She discovered that beauty was in the eye of the beholder, and everyone does not have to understand her. She learned the most important aspect of growth was to love herself, be herself and not give two shits what another soul had to say. This happens to be a product of said growth. Enjoy. (Insert Heart)

-SHE / HER

Fell in Love in the Zone

Times when I'm lost and filled with despair
I grab my pen and pad and it takes me there
I drop into this fantasy
blue skies, white clouds, no tears, and no fears
I imagine no cares
a free mind wandering with the ink
a freeness so rooted
i cant help but sink
into this fairy land
this beautiful region
no darkness just fluorescent illusions
astonishing me but brings no confusion
though my perfect world only last while I'm in the zone
it gives me this familiar high .. becomes my home
I've found my soulmates in this pad and this pen
a connection that will never end

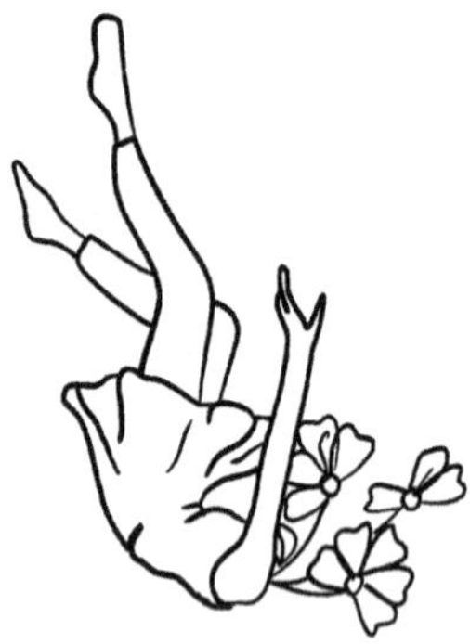

Unsolved Puzzle

Peace always seems to be the missing piece
imagine a mind always wondering never free
not letting go of troubles
has been my most burdensome disease
consuming my body, anemic, forceless, flimsy
peace is a puzzle and i'm missing pieces
struggling to become whole
searching for the lost deep down in my soul
freedom of the mind i'm undeniably lacking
impossible to be free in a constant mental prison
inner peace is absent leaving distress and
frustration
i'm inquiring a life of serenity to be free..
quiet, calm, and collective
i need that in me

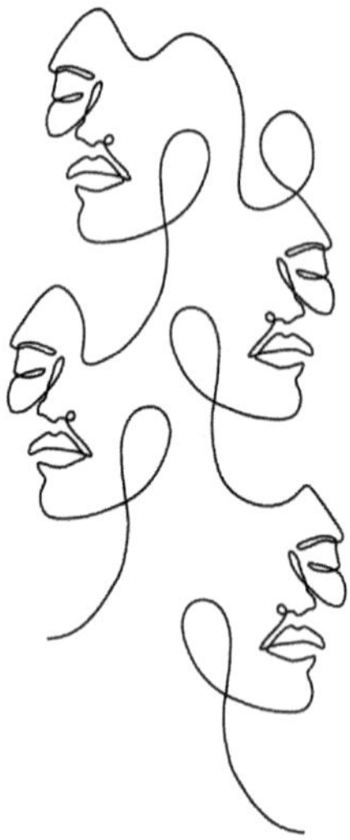

Mind Vs. Heart

Pieces of me scattered randomly in areas
where my mind just won't give in
making it impossible to find my own peace
within

as my heart starts to freeze
my mind works harder
to maintain the illusion my heart is getting
warmer
when in all actuality my heart has gone darker
than the sight of the visionless and only getting
colder

hard to gain mental peace
with the constant battle between the gloominess
in my chest verses the hopeful antics in my head
leading me to believe my heart has grown
a shade closer to red..

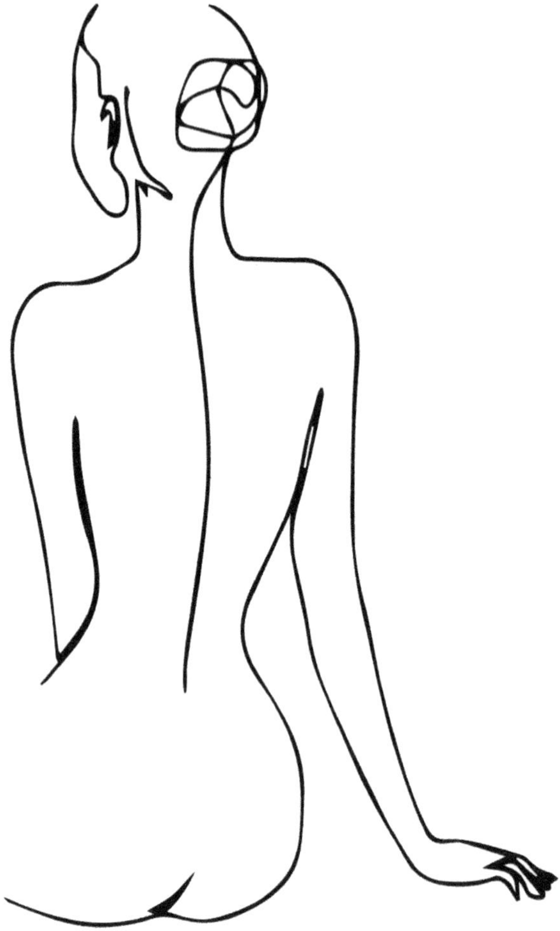

Relentless thoughts I can't control
fathomless feelings I cant console
fulfill my addiction
conclude my obsession

-it's starting

Empress Energy

Her depth was similar to the oceans
her love was just as deep
explains the reason why her vibrations
flow as waves do
and she has this subtle way of soothing you

Word Clouds

You have the ability to feed me things
my mind and soul are starving for
undressing me slowly with words
that enter my mentals and fondle my emotions
a majestic high that lifts my spirits
to a hallucinatory state
the more you speak the higher I sore
each word you articulate forms as
a cloud of protection
never letting me hit the floor

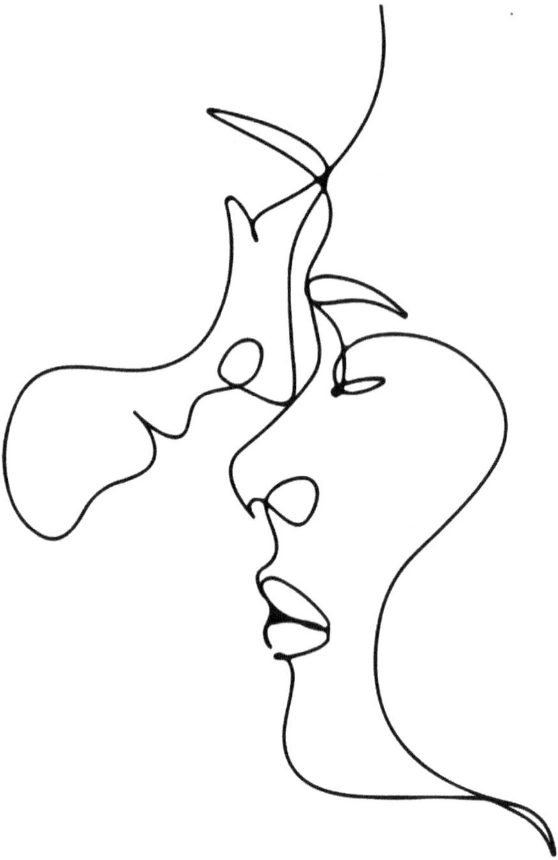

Twin Soul

Have you ever looked at someone and every single feature on them is beautiful?
You can't help but stare and get lost in every faucet of this individual. Lose yourself in their eyes every time you make eye contact for too long. Their voice is your favorite song on repeat, and you never get tired of hearing it.
Their smile makes your insides flutter with excitement. Every time they are with you it feels safe. Begin in their presence feels like home.
Love. At this moment I realized we were once one soul.

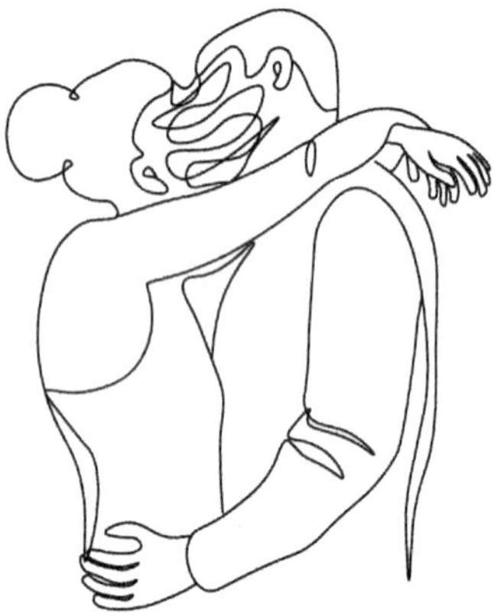

When I'm with you I vibrate higher
the way you stimulate my mentals
with your words drives me insane
yet every word serves as
a tonic to my insanity

-Good Fix

Baby's Stoned

Started out grounded
feet steady mind sober
then I consumed you
now I'm soaring high mind gone
but despite the fear I'll fly
inhaled your vibes
now I'm ascending to the stars
my favorite place by far
I'm floating there
slowly gliding through the air
inhaled your love
now I'll never come down
inhaled your affection
so I'll never touch the ground
euphoric high on cloud 9
I'd rather be stoned for the rest of my life.

Queen Me

I've never felt a love so rare
every piece of me is at peace
when you're near
the dominance of your character
influences me to be stronger
molding every part of me
understanding I'm nothing less than royalty
Tamed by my king I'll never let this go
feels like a dream ill never awake from
you seem to conquer every part of me
for that you've become my master
I'll always submit but with strength
to prove I can lead as well as follow
you're breaking down walls I built long ago
showing me its okay to love harder than before
ill never leave your side king
you've proven that your love for me
is on a whole different level
I trust that you'll protect my heart
and never let me fall apart
my respect for you is limitless
I have fully given you me
as this love is free

I always told myself I wish to be free
free of any strongholds or of any other
soul attempting to keep me stagnant.
The familiarity of being confined by
no choice of my own reminds me of
why its so important that I maintain my
freedom...
Then we crossed paths
While in your presence
I felt nothing but comfort in my own skin
Peace spewing from within
a fullness I've never experienced.
a supplemental amount of bliss
My heart smiled for the first time
yet trembled in fear and the sensation
was so unfamiliar. It's a hopeful fear
a peaceful fear and out of curiosity
I refuse to let fear have any reign.
I fantasize about making you feel safe,
feel free and feel unconditionally loved.
I imagine giving you a place
where you can safely experience any and all
emotions without feeling as though
you're giving away your power
without feeling as though you're losing control
I daydream about giving you every ounce
of my soul and essence known as me

sharing with you my freedom and
never taking yours away
providing structure without the cage.

-Freedom with you smells like Daffodils

Love is Light

in all different forms
unconditional Love
self Love
universal Love
romantic Love
be the Love you want to see in the world
Love heals
God is Love
we are Love
Love is Love

-Love 11(x)

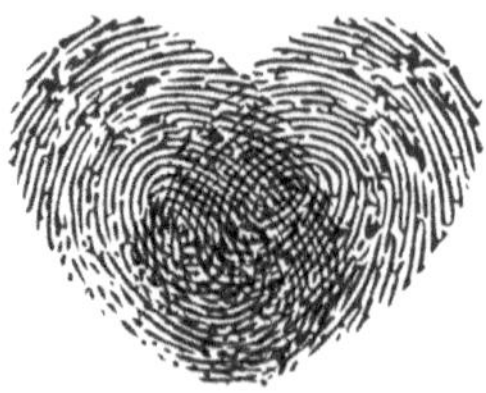

A flower growing peacefully through the dirt
pushing through when you want to give up hope
a smile even though you may hurt
finding peace when life is full of noise
loving yourself when others can't see your worth
spreading love even though your heart may be
broken
happiness when you are full of bliss
tears when you are full of sadness
finding the lessons in every inch of pain you
endure
having the courage to step up
even though you are scared of what's next
showing strength at your weakest point
never giving up on yourself

-All things Beautiful

Hurricane B

I wonder if he knows how it feels
to be broken over and over
when all you ever wanted was pure love
when all you wanted was to love another
soul within the depths of your every being
He must not know the gallons of tears you cry
every night feeling as though
you'll never be enough (for him) whether he's
right next to you or far away
He must think you're strong enough
to withstand any storm
especially those hurricanes that shoot down
lightning bolts filled with pain
those strong winds that cause destruction
to even the strongest structures
He must think the strength you
carry is out of this world
compliment or carelessness? I cant really tell
All I know is after this hurricane It'll take years
of rebuilding and reconstruction to bring
her world back to it's beautiful existence
the beauty she carried before the storm hit
is all she's longing for. A heart that's whole
Nothing More.

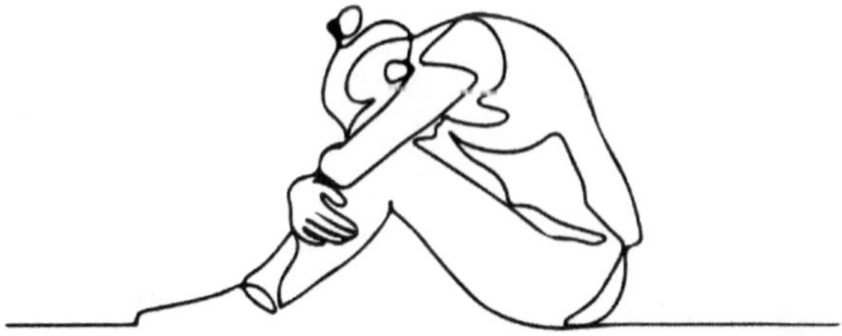

Now that you're gone
I rather stay asleep
because you
appear so vividly
in every single dream...

-Baffled

Unsettling Calm

I politely asked for my heart back
but you have it held captive
with no intention of giving it life
of pumping into it the blood
it needs to survive
so I ask why? no response
its like maybe you need it
more than i to keep your soul alive
Because anytime i vibrate
its at an all time high
and because of the strength I possess
I don't mind giving life to another soul
who may struggle to survive
I'll remain vital even if you expect me
to become listless eventually
the longer it's held captive
the more I'm introduced to the lioness in me
I guess you can keep it for as long as you need.

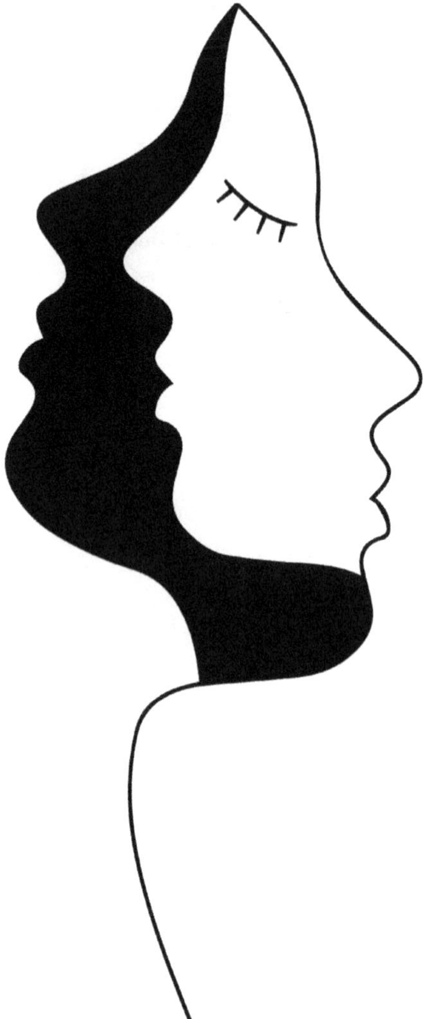

Fell in Love with a Dream....

the could haves
maybes
and everything in between
at times I rebreak my own heart
listening to songs that remind me of you
realizing how incapable you are of love
or that maybe you are capable...
just not able to love me

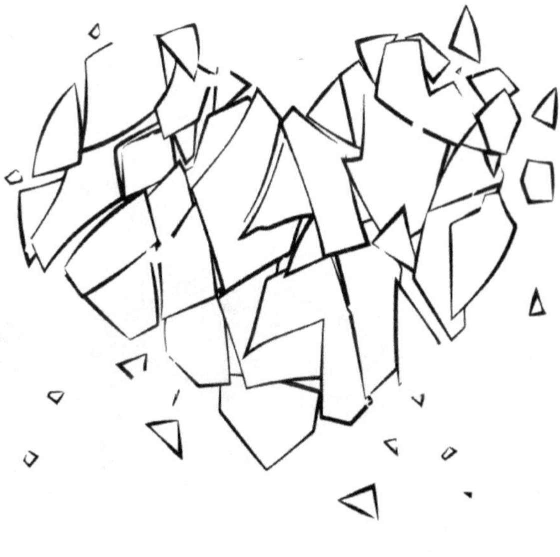

Was i enough?

Way to insecure to interpret any feels as real
instead I keep my heart packaged and sealed
its refusing to give you the love you deserve
and my mind won't let my heart give in to your
words
the ones you repeat so easily
the ones that make my body cringe
because you seem so sincere
yet my insecurities block every word
like a barricade so nothing's clear

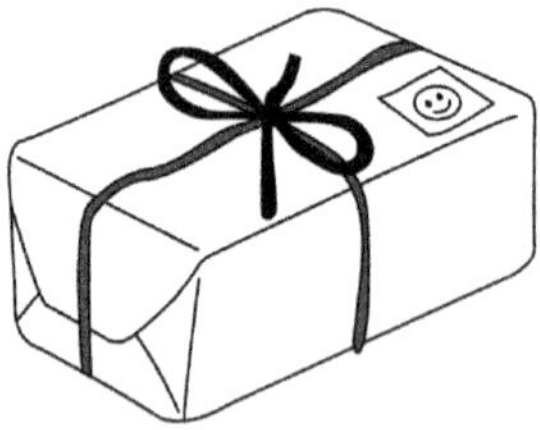

Haiku Love

Pure bliss found in peace,
Self love seeping though each pore,
Now she's glowing more.

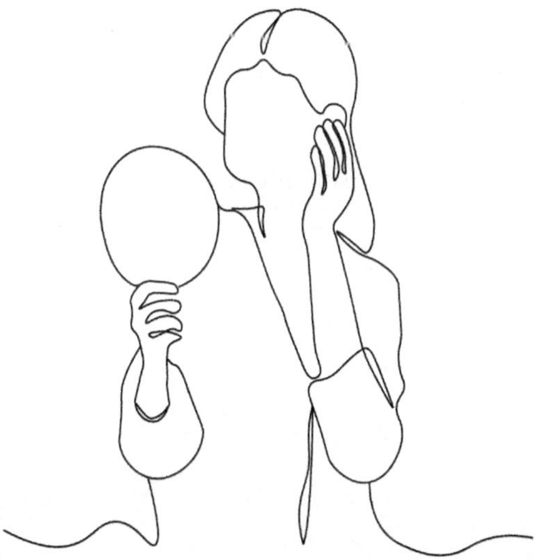

She is becoming..
With eloquence in the way she speaks..
She knows her love is too rare
to settle for unrequited intimacy.
She desires a connection
that lights her soul on fire
and stimulates her mentally..
She has so much self love
she sees right through any insincerities...
So she continues to live life
getting to know herself more..
She spends a lot of time in solitude
where she learns to listen to her heart and soul.
She is not at all lonely
only yearning for something Pure,
unconditional, and free.
Which is exactly what true love is supposed to be...

-To understand your worth

Spoke into existence
the love that she's been missing
Love of self was distant
now she's saturated in it
what you seek
Seeks you
Seek Love

-Manifesting

www.ingramcontent.com/pod-product-compliance
Lightning Source LLC
Chambersburg PA
CBHW051751130826
49812CB00033B/1107
* 9 7 8 9 3 5 7 2 1 1 4 0 6 *